Table of Contents

About the Author and Her Books. 4

1. How Do I Start?. 5
2. How Do I Know if My Writing Is Marketable?. 6
3. What Is the Best Format for Sending It?. 7
4. How Do I Make a Good First Impression?. 9
5. Should I Send Art Work?. 14
6. Why Should I Make a Picture Book Dummy?. 15
7. How Do I Grab and Keep a Reader's Interest?. 16
8. What Are Guidelines for Writing Nonfiction?. 22
9. What about Other Kinds of Writing?. 26
10. Should I Pay to Have a Book Published?. 27
11. What Should I Know about Copyright?. 29
12. What Should I Do about Record Keeping?. 30
13. How Can I Increase Sales after Publication?. 31
14. What's Next?. 32

Appendix A 33
Appendix B 35
Index. 38

About the Author

Betsy Blizzard Lee has worked as a children's author, a school psychologist, a school counselor, and a rehabilitation counselor. She is a member of the Society of Children's Book Writers and Illustrators. She has written stories for magazines and for use in educational software. She teaches college classes about writing and selling stories written for children.

Other Publications by the Author

Little Lemon: Activities for Developing Motivation and Memory Skills is a K - 3 book with a fictional story, discussion questions, lesson plans, activities, and music. Puppets can be purchased separately. The materials were developed for school and home use to help children learn *how to* learn more effectively.

A Purple Cow: How to Learn Colors is a Pre-K -3 book which has an easy way to teach colors. Beyond that, it offers learning strategies which benefit children who have difficulty learning colors. It has a fictional story with Little Lemon, music, and hands-on activities.

A Funny Dolch Word Book #1: Stories, Poems, Word Puzzles uses all of the pre-primer, primer, and first grade Dolch sight words in the text plus many of them on this level in the word puzzles.

10,000 White Horses is a story of a child catching the horses of the foam as she rides a wave to shore with 10,000 white horses and more.

Author's Web Site

Visit Breezy Bits for more information about the author and her books. http://www.geocities.com/labooks.geo

Ordering Information

An order form is on the inside back cover of this book.

1. How Do I Start?

Think of why you want to write for children. What do you want to say to them? Do you want to entertain, inspire, or inform? Do you want to help children with concerns you had as a child? Have you been moved by a scene or an incident which is best expressed in this genre? What age person do you want to hear your story? Do you enjoy reading the little pearls of wisdom, breezy bits of entertainment, and concise presentations of information which are written for children?

Read this book before you begin to write or before you continue to write a story you have started. Learn about planning, plotting, etc.

Begin writing by following your plan and getting your story down on paper using minimal (or no) correcting as you go. If you are mostly an auditory learner, you might record the story as you tell it. Then write it down. Check spelling, grammar, and clarity. Work on other techniques you are learning. Most writers see each new story with a thrill of love for the new baby. Put it aside for a few weeks unless it is for a course. Later, try to see it in a more objective light.

Writer's block hits most writers from time to time. If the paper remains blank, you might write about whatever you are thinking. I did this once with a sonnet which ended: "So now, I'll don my handy thinking bonnet, and settle down to write my little sonnet."

This can get words started but it can waste time if it is overdone. Do research. Read children's books. Observe children. Add to your journal. Work on another part of the story, perhaps the ending.

Realize that our minds work well on unfinished tasks if we take *short, non-stimulating* breaks. Take a short walk, eat an apple, pet the dog, or dust the furniture. Be sure that your breaks aren't just a way of putting off doing what you need to do — write and revise.

Keep a note pad and pencil with you. Sometimes you might even wake up in the night and jot down an idea.

2. How Do I Know if My Writing Is Marketable?

Taking a course from someone with writing experience gives you valuable feedback. You will polish your skills and learn about helpful techniques and resources.

Share what you have written. When you write for children, you have three audiences: today's children, adults, and the child you used to be. Get valuable feedback from parents, teachers, librarians, other writers, and children. Even editors might offer encouragement which you do not notice. There is more about that later.

I find it encouraging to read in classrooms. If you do this, I suggest that you have the teacher stay in the room. You need the reactions of the teacher and the children. Also, you should not be put in the role of being a substitute teacher. Know your story well enough to have almost constant eye contact with your audience. Get a feeling for their reactions. I recall adding something funny to a story while reading it as I interacted with my audience.

When you read your story, you put a lot of your personality into the reading. For a more objective view, have someone else read your story out loud. They might hesitate over something which you thought read smoothly. Their inflections might give an impression which is different from what you intended. If an adult plans to read it to children, have the adult read it to you first in case there are any problems of this type which need to be revised.

When asking for feedback, avoid vague words like good and bad. Mention working on stories to make them better. Some questions are:
1. What did you like about the story?
2. Are there some things that it would be OK to leave out?
3. What do you think would make the story better?

Feedback is important but remember to keep your own style or voice. Develop a feeling for when to stop revising and when to send your *baby* out into the world.

3. What Is the Best Format for Sending It?

The following is copied with permission from **The Society of Children's Book Writers and Illustrators. (SCBWI)** Contact info is in Appendix A.

"From Typewriter to Printed Page...Facts You Need to Know"

The Form of a Manuscript

In general, all manuscripts submitted to legitimate publishing houses, whether sent in by agents or submitted directly by you, *are read* — except those which are handwritten. There is a proper form that a manuscript should take. It is to your advantage to have your manuscript follow this form so that it looks as professional as possible. The following guidelines should be followed when submitting a manuscript to a publisher:

If you use a typewriter:

*Use a good weight white paper, 8 ½" by 11."

*Type double-spaced, with no more than 25 lines to the page (except the first page, which is shorter). Allow margins of at least 1" on each side of the paper.

*Neatness is of the essence. Retype pages containing strike-overs and include as few erasures as possible.

*ALWAYS keep a carbon or clean photocopy of every manuscript that you submit to a publisher.

*Number each page consecutively in the top right-hand corner with the exception of the first page which is not numbered.

*Include on every page (with the exception of the first page) your last name and a key word from the title. This information should go in the upper left-hand corner.

If you use a word processor:

*Margins, spacing, and form are the same as the typewritten page.

*Dot-matrix is the least desirable type of printer. Some publishers refuse to read manuscripts submitted in dot-matrix print because it is difficult to read. Daisy wheel, thimble, laser, and ink jet printers are all acceptable. In all cases, be sure you use a fresh black ribbon.

*Select an IBM or easy-to-read style of type such as Courier 10 or Courier 72. Avoid elaborate or script type styles.

*Use 20 lb. computer paper. For continuous feed printers, use laser edge paper which tears smoothly. If you use a tractor feed printer to print your manuscripts, tear off the holes on the sides, and tear the pages apart. Do not send your disk unless the publisher requests it.

*Keep one hard copy and your disk. Don't reuse the disk until after the book or article is published. Check with the publisher before reformatting the disk for a new manuscript.

The format of the first page should conform to the following specifications.

Your name
Your address
Your city, state, zip

        TITLE ALL IN CAPS (half-way down page)

        By Your Name

        Your story begins here. (3/4 way down the page)

Below is an example of specifications of other pages. Your last name/key word from the title   Page #
(at the top left corner)   (at the top right corner)

4. How Do I Make a Good First Impression?

Check resources such as *The Children's Writer's & Illustrator's Market*. Does the publisher use this kind of material? Is it for a book or a magazine publisher? It might be appropriate as a book if:
1. You have at least 20 illustration possibilities which will hold interest and help move the story along;
2. You would be willing to pay from $10 to $15 for it;
3. Children will want to read or hear it again and again;
4. Adults will want to read it to children again and again.

The following is copied with permission from **The Society of Children's Book Writers and Illustrators. (SCBWI)** Contact info is in Appendix A.

"From Typewriter to Printed Page...Facts You Need to Know"

NUMBER OF MANUSCRIPT PAGES

While there are no specific requirements (nor should there be) for any kind of book, a survey of many published SCBWI members indicated ranges of manuscript pages that are suitable and saleable.

Taking into consideration that your main character has the greatest influence on how your manuscript will be viewed (i.e. if your main character is a chipmunk, it is not likely that your manuscript will be suitable for young adults), and remembering that *there are exceptions to everything*, the following are the number of manuscript pages *most often cited* by the respondents to the survey. Please, use this only as a *guide* not an absolute.

Genre of Book	Number of Manuscript Pages
Board Book	½ -1
Picture Book	2-3
Picture Story Book	6-9

Some respondents indicated that they had done longer picture books (5-10 pages) and picture story books (up to 15 pages) but recognized that "shorter is better" when a book is to be illustrated.

Genre of Book	Number of Manuscript Pages
Easy-reader Book	10-20
Young Middle-grade Fiction	40-60

This genre produced the most variance in the survey; manuscripts of 20 pages were reported, as were manuscripts of 125 pages.

Middle-grade Novels	100-150
YA Novels	175-200

This genre produced the least variance; 200 pages were cited more often than any other.

Young Nonfiction	10-20
Middle-grade Nonfiction	60-100
YA Nonfiction	100-150
Romance Novels	140-160
Poetry/Verse for Young Readers	15-40
Poetry/Verse for Older Readers	50-150

In manuscript, poems/verses are one each page.

SUBMITTING THE MANUSCRIPT

Before sending your manuscript to a publisher, you need to determine which publishing houses publish the kind of material you are submitting. A careful investigation of publishers' catalogues (available on request from the publisher), CHILDREN'S BOOKS IN PRINT (available in the library), various marketing lists found in writers' periodicals, and most importantly, examination of the books themselves should indicate to you which publishing houses would be most receptive to your work.

*Manuscripts should be addressed to an editor in the juvenile department. The names of editors are listed in the LITERARY MARKET PLACE (available in the library) and in some writers' periodicals.

*ALWAYS include a self-addressed, stamped envelope of the correct size to hold your manuscript with a sufficient amount of postage.

*It is advisable to include a cover letter. However, it should be brief. Include only information which is necessary for the editor to know as relates to your manuscript; e.g. if nonfiction, how are you qualified to discuss your subject, or if fiction, a brief mention of your publishing credits. If you are submitting your manuscript in response to a previous query, mention this in your cover letter. The cover letter should never try to explain the story. Your story must speak for itself.

*Keep copies of all correspondence.

*Unless you are a professional illustrator, do not include illustrations with your manuscript.

*Do not attempt to indicate where you would like illustrations to be placed in your story, or what they should portray. This is the province of the editor and the illustrator.

*Some publishers will send you a letter or post card acknowledging receipt of your manuscript, but others will not. You may wish to include a self-addressed stamped postcard with your manuscript.

*A decision on your manuscript may take three months or more. Some editors are slower to respond than others. To shorten the time you have to wait, the SCBWI recommends that you submit a copy of your manuscript rather than the original (note in your cover letter that it is a copy). If you have not had a response at the end of two months, send a polite letter of inquiry to the editor asking about the status of your manuscript. If you have still not heard at the end of three months, write to the editor — withdrawing your manuscript from consideration — and submit another copy elsewhere. You may or may not get your first submitted copy back, but you need not worry — no publisher will use it without your knowledge and permission.

*Submitting manuscripts to several publishers at the same time (a policy called multiple submissions) is frowned upon by most juvenile book editors. Those editors who do accept multiple submissions must be told that it is such. The SCBWI does not recommend multiple submissions.

All submissions must be accompanied by a self-addressed, stamped return envelope. (SASE)

RESPONDING TO EDITORIAL NOTES/LETTERS

The intention of a penned note on a form rejection or a personal letter from an editor is to let the writer know that the editor is interested in the writer's work.

*If there is a penned note on a rejection, i.e. "Try us again" or some such, the proper response is a short, polite letter thanking the editor for his/her interest and expressing the hope that a new manuscript from you will better suit his/her needs. If you have a new manuscript, send it with the letter. Make sure, however, that it is appropriate for that publisher and that it is the best work of which you are capable.

*If you have received a personal letter, detailing some revision suggestions, but not promising a contract, the proper response is a letter to the editor thanking him/her for the time and interest given to your manuscript. Then consider the editor's suggestions carefully. If you decide that your manuscript would indeed be improved by those revisions and do them, you are professionally obligated to send that manuscript back to that editor (no editor spends time to write a detailed editorial letter without expecting to see the manuscript again); be sure to mention, in your letter accompanying the revised manuscript, that you have followed the editor's suggestions for revisions. However, if you decide not to revise the manuscript as suggested, do not plan to send it back to that editor. Send it elsewhere.

QUERY LETTERS

It is generally a good idea to query a publisher before submitting nonfiction material. Query letters should include the subject matter, the age group for which you intend it, and the reason that your book will be different from competing books on the subject already in existence. (Research on competing books is best begun by consulting the SUBJECT GUIDE TO CHILDREN'S BOOKS IN PRINT, and then examining those books). Many juvenile book editors wish to be sent a query before submitting novel length fiction material. Some editors will wish to see an outline/synopsis and a chapter or two as well.

AGENTS

Many writers of adult and juvenile books do not choose to be represented by an agent. An agent is not necessary to sell a saleable manuscript. However, if you wish to be represented by an agent, these are some things you should know.

*Not all agents handle juvenile material. A list of those who do is available to SCBWI members.

*Often, it is difficult to get an agent if you have not made previous sales on your own.

*Agents should be sent a query letter before manuscripts are sent to them. A SASE must be included.

*The SCBWI recommends that you be cautious when dealing with agents who charge a reading fee.

SUBSIDY PUBLISHERS

Publishers who ask you to pay for publication of your work (subsidy or vanity publishers) should be avoided completely.

MAGAZINES

Submitting manuscripts to juvenile magazines is in some ways different from submitting to book publishers. Some of these differences are:

*The first page of a manuscript should include in the upper right-hand corner the approximate word count (rounded off to the nearest ten).

*Magazine publishers generally do not acknowledge receipt of manuscripts.

*It is appropriate to inquire about your manuscript after two months have elapsed.

*Some magazines, especially in the religious field, will accept multiple submissions.

*Most agents will not handle magazine sales.

*Magazines plan issues far in advance. It is important to keep this in mind when submitting seasonal material.

*Some magazines pay on publication. They may hold your manuscript for a considerable length of time before either printing it or returning it. The SCBWI recommends that magazines that pay on publication be placed on the bottom of your list as possible publishers of your work.

*Most juvenile magazines do not pay large amounts for their material, but they can provide the novice writer with invaluable experience.

5. Should I Send Art Work?

Unless you plan to be the illustrator, do not submit art work. Publishers prefer to team an unknown author with an experienced illustrator. This can increase the chances of sales.

Great art work won't make up for a poorly written story. If you submit art work and text, one might be accepted and the other rejected. That might be good if you are the author-illustrator; but if you have teamed up with a friend, this could create a problem.

Author-illustrators send a few sketches and a color copy of one finished picture. Do not send originals. If you are willing to illustrate other people's work, mention this in the cover letter.

Some books depend on having the art portray parts of the story which are not in the text. You can note in the manuscript what ideas need to be conveyed, but leave room for the artist's creativity. In books which are heavily dependent on the art, you might send a dummy with stick figures. Type the text on the pages of the dummy. Send the manuscript in standard format, also. For a non-artist, a dummy should only be sent if the author has an unusual twist that needs visual help, and can *not* make it clear in a cover letter alone. More information about this is in *How to Write a Children's Book and Get It Published* by Barbara Seuling. (Appendix B)

Unless part of the story needs to be shown by illustrations, do not mention the placement or content of illustrations. However, you should double space twice to indicate page breaks.

Authors and illustrators do not usually communicate, but here is how one team worked. For *Annushka's Voyage* by Edith Tarbescu, a cover letter indicated that the story was about her mother and aunt in the early 1900's. The immigrants wore name tags. For inspiration, the illustrator requested photos of the women in their youth. At the editor's request, Edith supplied an author's note with historical details. This and the photo were used in the back of the book.

6. Why Should I Make a Picture Book Dummy?

Even though you do not send a dummy to the publisher, there are several reasons for making one. The creation of a dummy is to help you fine tune your writing. First, write your story concentrating on character, plot, action, etc. Then think in terms of illustration possibilities and what the text will be on each two-page spread. Is there something on the spread which would make a good picture? Does each spread help move the story along? Each spread should end with something which makes the reader want to turn the page rather than to put the book down. The emotional tone of the two pages should blend. If happiness is the tone but something sad is about to happen, wait till the page turns for it to happen. Are there too many words on a two-page spread? Are there about 20 good illustration possibilities? Do they offer variety and action?

The average picture book has 32 pages. Books are printed on signatures. A signature is a large sheet of paper which is fed into the press. A 16-page signature has eight pages on each side. An entire 32-page book is printed on two of these signatures. The signature is folded, trimmed, and bound.

For a better idea of the flow of your story and the limited amount of text, create an eight-page signature by folding an 8 ½" by 11" paper twice. Use four sheets (four eight-page signatures) for a 32-page dummy. Trim, bind, and number the pages. Use tape or a glue stick to put your typed text on the appropriate pages. You will probably need to move or delete some text. The pages are easier to handle if you cut them and put them in a folder using page protectors.

The text usually starts on page three. The first pages are the title page and the copyright page. For your working dummy, think of text from page 3-16, or 3-32, and so forth in multiples of eight.

Barbara Seuling's book has more about making dummies. Jean Karl's book has many details about picture books. (Appendix B)

7. How Do I Grab and Keep a Reader's Interest?

Are you writing because a character, situation, location, or time period interests you? Think of why it interests you, and use the following techniques to gain and keep your reader's interest.

<u>Themes</u>
Fiction entertains. Memorable fiction has themes (basic truths). The theme is the topic and your opinion about the topic. It can be stated in one sentence or phrase, such as — the value of the work ethic. The theme is shown through the interaction of your characters. It is not stated outright. For example in *The Little Red Hen,* the hen shared the fruits of her labor with her chicks, but she refused to share with capable adults who refused to work.

<u>Plot</u>
How is theme different from plot? The plot is the series of events leading to the conclusion.
Writing is like taking a trip. *If you don't know where or why you are going, how will you know when you have arrived?*
Make a rough <u>outline</u> to keep you from wasting time wandering aimlessly. You need a basic idea of *who* is going, *why* they are going, *who* is going with them, *where* and *when* they are going, and *how* they will get there. *What* obstacles and adventures they will meet? *What* is the <u>crisis</u> where things cannot get any worse? The <u>climax</u> follows the crisis. It is the moment of truth — *what* final choice is made or *what* insight is gained by the main character. *How* has this happened? Your character reaches the goal or chooses a new acceptable, direction. Answer these questions. Who? Why? Where? When? How? What?

<u>What's the main character's motivation</u>?
Children and adults are motivated by many needs: achievement, spirituality, power, knowledge, fun, forgiveness, etc.

Several decades ago, Abraham H. Maslow led the revolt against popular views of psychoanalysis and behaviorism. His hierarchal theory of needs emphasized the study of well-adjusted people rather than ones found in clinical practice. (Good and Brophy, Appendix B)

1. Physiological needs (sleep, thirst, relief from pain, etc.)
2. Safety needs (physical and psychological)
3. Love (acceptance; belonging to a peer group, family, etc.)
4. Esteem (from mastery experiences; self-respect, not conceit)
5. Self-actualization (highest human potential, creativity, a search for meaningfulness, improvements to society)

Maslow felt that more basic needs must be met before higher ones were achieved. Sometimes, the structure is dynamic, e.g. the dominant need can shift from safety to self-actualization.

Some people *interpret* self-esteem as feeling good about yourself regardless of your accomplishments or behavior. Maslow spoke of self-esteem which comes from accomplishments requiring effort. Remember this in story writing. If we *dumb down* the criteria, where is the glory in reaching the goal?

How important is the main character's goal?

The goal must be viewed by your character and readers as being worth the effort. Any eight-year-old child can tie a bow. There's no story. Who cares! What if the child has Down's syndrome? How does the child feel about being two years behind average? Does the child notice? Does tying the bow spark the confidence to try other things? As you develop your story, often ask yourself, *what if*.

Whose story is it?

What if the child with Down's syndrome doesn't seem to care and makes few efforts to achieve? There's no story. Wait. What if the dad is determined to motivate the child? You might have a story with a possible conflict, but whose story is it?

The first step in writing is deciding whose story you are telling. If you write about the dad's need to help the child, it is the dad's story (goals, struggles, and accomplishments). The dad's story might be a story for adults rather than for children. The reader must be able to identify with the main character's efforts to solve the problem.

Traits

What traits does the main character need to accomplish the goal? Some traits could be physical strength, the knack for gaining the cooperation of others, or knowledge, e.g. a child's experience with batteries but not with cars sparks the idea of cleaning the battery's connections on the stranded car for just enough power to get home.

Use plants to make the reader aware of some traits before they are needed to solve the problem. Suppose you never had heard of Superman and were reading the first book about him. You expect him to be super because of his name. You learn that he does superhuman things and that he cares about people. It does not jolt you out of the story and back to reality when he flies to rescue someone. You accept these traits as part of the story. Surprises are needed but the foundation needs to be laid.

A trait needed for problem solving *might* be shown by illustrations rather than by the text. In *The Digging-est Dog* by Al Perkins, a rescue was made by creating a dog chain. Each dog grabbed the tail of the one ahead. The chain of dogs was lowered into the well to rescue Duke. The trait might be an essential feature which does not need to be mentioned in the text. We knew the dogs had tails! However, we did not expect them to be used this way. The artist was careful to give them long tails. The main character was rescued from the well although everyone was angry at him. This was the major crisis of the story, i.e. the point at which things could not get any worse. After being rescued, Duke had an important choice to make.

A plant can be an item which is needed at the end of the story, e.g. a cell phone. Include it earlier without making it seem important.

Point or foreshadow

Suggest that certain things might happen. A character says, "You'd better not do that," or says, "This sure is spooky." A storm is approaching, or one shoe is found.

Tags

Tigger bounces. Linus hugs his blanket. We are not told that Tigger is energetic and Linus is insecure. Tags are basic identifying marks so all characters will not seem the same or flat. One character might often look at a watch. One might have long, straight, red hair. A tag shows a character trait or an aspect of appearance.

Dialogue tags are words such as *said*. Vary them some, but do it when you need to emphasize how the words are said. Think literally. Can you smile or laugh a sentence? Instead of writing, "I like it," she laughed. Try writing, her eyes sparkled as she said, "I like it." Or try, "I like It." (Period) She laughed. (Wyndham Appendix B)

SDT

Show don't tell. Do not end with, "And they'll never, never do it again." You need to show a change, but do not overdo it.

Show feelings through actions. We know Tigger's traits by his usual behavior. If he hugs a security blanket, we know something is wrong. We want to know about the *out of character* behavior.

Show actions rather than tell about them. "The dog ran down the driveway to see Susie." This tells about it. "The cocker spaniel's ears bounced as he trotted down the driveway to Susie, jumped into her lap, and wagged his stubby tail." We see it.

Visualize each scene. Be sure Susie is not *standing* in the driveway if the dog jumps into her lap.

Viewpoint

When writing for children and teenagers, it is best to use the single viewpoint told in first or third person. There are other viewpoints used by writers for adults, such as the omniscient viewpoint. Readers know how several characters feel by seeing things through the eyes and feelings of different characters.

This does not work for children. Your readers learn about how others feel through what the main character learns. She or he sees others smiling, frowning, etc. Everything your readers see, hear, smell, taste, touch, feel, or know is shown through the main character's experiences. Use the single viewpoint and stay with it.

Perspective

Remember how it felt to have a dog look you in the eye when you were standing up? Sit on the floor. Try it with a St. Bernard.

Remember how children think. Stories can help children mature, but trying to rush perception can be futile or a blow to confidence. It takes time to grow up. Here's a true story about a young art teacher who tried to rush a 6-year-old child's coloring skills by saying, "Fill in the space between the sky and the ground. Look out the window at that mountain. See how the sky comes down to touch the top of the mountain?" The child shook her head and explained gently as if talking to a senile person. "I'm *very* sorry to tell you this, but I've *been* on top of that mountain and the sky doesn't touch it."

Observe children! Volunteer at school, church, scouts, etc. Read books about typical behavior at different ages. Jean Piaget and others have written about children's perceptions. (Appendix B)

Start the story quickly.

Begin with an action, pose a question, arouse curiosity. Who is the main character? What does he or she need? As the writer, you should know the motivation even if it is not shown until the end. Study the beginnings of stories.

Conflict

The middle of the story has a series of ups and downs. Your main character must be the one dealing with opposition and must be the one solving the problem or reaching the goal.

External conflicts can be a struggle against other people, nature, robots, etc. Especially for older children, use internal and external conflicts in the same story.

Internal or inner conflicts involve a situation in which the main character makes a difficult choice between demands or desires that are incompatible with each other. Gestalt psychologist, Kurt Lewin, presented this description of inner conflicts. (Reese, Appendix B)

Approach-approach (Both choices are desired, but this is not really a *win-win* situation. In order to be a conflict, the choice must result in eliminating or significantly delaying the other options.)

Approach-avoidance (There are positive and negative feelings about the same object, person, or situation like a love-hate situation, or a favorable outcome with some unfavorable side-effects.)

Avoidance-avoidance (This is a lose-lose situation. There is a choice between two equally undesirable demands.)

How will your main character resolve conflicts?

Villain
The villain needs to be a real challenge. Younger children tend to think of characters as being all good or all bad - the super hero and the worthless villain. In more believable stories, the villain has a decent feature or two and the hero or heroine has some human flaws.

It isn't over till it's over.
Keep the *middle* of the story moving. Give the reader some doubts until the very end as to whether or how the goal can be accomplished.

Sometimes, the goal needs to be abandoned by the main character with a decision to aim for something else because the initial goal turns out to be unrealistic. A new and more worthy goal needs to emerge in the natural course of events. He or she comes to terms with making the better of two choices in a difficult situation. Your reader must be left with the feeling that this was the right thing to do.

Significance
To avoid a *slight* story, your main character shows some growth. It can be some little insight about himself/herself or about other people, pets, or life. It can be improved confidence from accomplishing something difficult. Show how the character feels.

When it's over, stop!
In some ways, a good story is like a well-told joke where you build up to a climax and deliver the punch line. After the punch line, there is no need or point in explaining. All of the pieces should *fall* into place. If you feel a need to explain a joke, it probably means that you told it to the wrong audience or you didn't make an adequate presentation. You should not try to explain a story.

In a story, it is over when the climax and the struggle are done. The pieces suddenly *fall* into place. Having the pieces *fall* into place doesn't just happen. It is the result of careful planning and writing (or telling) of a joke or a story. In a story, there is a brief resolution for a feeling of completeness. Be sure to close with the main character's thoughts, feelings, or actions. Stories for children and teens should end on a positive or on a hopeful note.

Study the last few pages or the last chapter of favorite books.

8. What Are Guidelines for Writing Nonfiction?

The nonfiction market is large. If the topic is popular, there is often a need for a book for a different age group or one with a different slant for the same age group. New developments take place creating a need for books about a topic which has not been covered much.

Before researching a topic, study the market's need for it. Do we have enough books about learning the ABC's for instance? Visit the library. Review *The Subject Guide to Children's Books-in-Print.* Talk with children's librarians and teachers. Read publishers' guidelines.

Think about things which interest you. Select a topic which would also interest children. Could a variety of interesting pictures help deal with the subject? Can you help a child gain some new understanding or knowledge of the subject?

Think of the background information needed for children of different ages. Remember the perceptual development for different ages. Younger children have little concept of the differences in 15 or 50 years. They can relate to *before grandmother was born*, etc.

Select an age group for which you want to write. If there is a large number of books available on the topic for this age group, do you have new information you can offer?

As you research, have a rough idea of how much information you want to cover. The complexity and amount depend on the age of the child. Accuracy is paramount for all ages. Make a rough outline. Decide what your major point will be and where to begin based on children's background knowledge and interests. Find out what is taught on this grade level about your topic. Do schools need books on the topic for remedial or enrichment materials? Develop a pattern in your outline. Do you want to lead from one stage or region to another? Do you want to present categories, such as breeds of horses? Will you use humor? Gather more information than needed.

Write, revise, then share with an expert. The information might be an entire story for magazines, nonfiction picture books, and concept books. It might be sample chapters and an outline for longer books. Follow the expert's suggestions about accuracy but maintain your own style of presentation of the material. After a book contract is signed, you might want to contact this person about an endorsement. You might share your story with a teacher or a librarian.

Keep track of where you get information: the book, article, author, pages or chapters, publisher with address, and maybe even if you got the material from the college library, town library, from a friend, etc. in case you need to go back to it. You do not use footnotes, but you can use statements such as this: in Seuling's book (Appendix B), she suggests.... Be sure to document the source and contact information of graphs or illustrations which you select. Permissions will be requested after your sale and before publication.

For older readers, you will need one appendix or more. It is helpful to include sources where readers can get free information.

Research publishers. *The Children's Writer's & Illustrator's Market* has subject listings, details about publishers, trends, etc. Consult the Publishers Weekly (in most libraries) for trends, etc.

Send a query letter. More information about queries for longer books is under <u>Books for older children and teens</u>. It is not necessary to send a query letter for nonfiction picture books and for concept books, however it could save time. The publisher might be working on a book for your topic and age group. There would not be a need to publish two similar books.

Do not overlook the magazine market. You could use some of the information you are collecting for short articles. This would be different from a chapter in your book.

Magazines have a variety of needs: seasonal materials, articles about items in the news, how-to articles about crafts and other topics, crossword puzzles, mazes, games, fillers (e.g. short jokes), poetry, etc. Check recent issues and current guidelines.

Compared to book editors, magazine editors are often more willing to take a chance on an unpublished writer or illustrator. They do not pay much as book publishers pay therefore the magazine's investment is small. The risk is almost non-existent. If readers are not thrilled with an article, puzzle, story, or whatever, they are very unlikely to cancel their subscriptions to the magazine.

On the other hand, a book publisher is making a large investment and taking the risk of not covering expenses with the first book by an unknown writer. You make a more favorable first impression on children's book editors if your work has been published in a magazine for children. In addition to good books, publishers want an author who is professional and who will help promote the book. Of course, the final decision will depend on their current needs and the quality of the manuscript.

Concept books

A nonfiction concept book explores topics directly and openly.

As an example, consider helping children deal with the fear of thunder. You can expect a strong reaction to thunder. An unexpected, loud noise will produce a startled response. If hearing is normal, this is a natural reaction from infancy throughout adulthood. Although the source of childhood fears might not be realistic, remain sensitive to the fact that the fears are very real.

Jean Karl (Appendix B) suggests three ways to avoid a preachy approach to your message. I have adapted her suggestions to the fear of thunder. You might use *humor* such as *exaggeration* or *silliness* regarding a fear. The window rattles like a drum and the child imitates the sound. Another approach would be to create a *mood of beauty and delight,* e.g. for the beauty of God's fireworks. You could take a *non-committal factual* approach, e.g. learn about what causes thunder. Learn to count the time lapse between seeing lightning and hearing thunder. Learn a little about lightning and safety measures regarding lightning.

Concept books deal with simple joys, struggles, appreciation, gaining knowledge, or many other needs and interests. Tap childhood emotions and sensitivity as you present the information.

In your outline for concept books, note approximately how many pages you want to devote to each idea. Children are curious. They want to learn, and they will enjoy a nonfiction book if your presentation of facts is interesting and if you supply enough background for them.

Fiction in concept books can explore the sensations such as those of a fresh garden after the rain — the sounds, smells, and sights. How do things feel to the touch? How do fresh blueberries taste when washed by the rain? These books can be informational, e.g. showing aspects of caring for a pet or exploring feelings about what it is like to be small.

Books for older children and teens

Query letters are necessary for books written for older children, and they can save you a lot of time and expense.

Your query letter should tell a little about you, e.g. how you are qualified to write about this topic. Mention experts who have checked the accuracy of your facts. If your work, travel, hobby, or volunteer experiences involve the topic, be sure to mention this. You do not have to be an expert. You might have a fresh angle even if you are not an expert.

If you get a positive response to your query, make a book proposal: a detailed outline with two or three chapters. The third chapter can be the last one in the book to show how you plan to end it. Some changes from the original outline are acceptable.

The outline can be formal with headings and subheadings. It can be a chapter by chapter outline, but use major topics and details under those topics. You may use incomplete sentences. Include a list of references and possibly sources for free material, e.g. organizations and web sites.

There is more about fiction for teens in chapters 7 and 9.

Books by Seuling, by Wyndham, and by others go into more details about writing fiction and nonfiction. (Appendix B)

Revise and polish letters as well as stories. Your letter is the very first impression you give. If you spill something on the letter, it is best to start over. Check for errors in spelling, etc.

9. What about Other Kinds of Writing?

In this book, information has been presented which is basic to all good writing for children and teenagers. In classes about writing for children, a wide variety of manuscripts for children and teens is critiqued. However, teaching about how to write for all genres in this field is beyond the scope of this text. Some of the resources in Appendix B deal with the following genres and many others. Check the subject guide in *The Children's Writer's and Illustrator's Market* for publishers in your interest areas.

Poetry and verse
   Editors have seen so much poorly done verse, the first impression often is negative. If you love to write poetry or verse, polish your skills well in this area. Your first sales might be to magazines and greeting card companies.

Novelty books and board books
   Many publishers do not carry these because expensive, special equipment is needed to produce them. You can find publishers for this type of book by visiting a bookstore. I typed *board books* into a search box at amazon.com and found several publishers. I did the same for *novelty books* and found a few publishers. I have not found a book dealing only with novelty books or board books.

Middle grade fiction and young adult fiction
   The main differences in these two types of books are the age of the main character, the nature of the conflict, and complexity of the plot. More information is at http://www.write4kids.com/ .

Easy readers
   Many publishers no longer use strictly controlled vocabulary lists. You need to be aware of the general reading level. The books have short sentences and a ragged right format (left justification of type).

10. Should I Pay to Have a Book Published?

If you are considering a vanity press or subsidy press, my answer is no. You pay to have the book published. They praise your writing and promise you the moon. What you get is more like moonshine. You have no control over quality; they often do not deliver as many books as promised; and they do little if any promotion.

Self-publishing is flourishing because of new technology, for example, desk top publishing and e-books. Another reason is that fewer people are deciding what books are available for the rest of us to read. Many companies have merged. Buyers for the five top chain stores control one-third of books sold. (Poynter, Appendix B)

If you are considering self-publishing, my answer is maybe. Self-publishers are in charge of everything and have the reputation for taking greater care with editing and other aspects of quality. Big publishers look for self-published books at The BookExpo America Book Fair sponsored by The American Booksellers Association. (Appendix A) Many distributors, wholesalers, and chain bookstores will not work with a beginning self-publisher, but you can start with independent bookstores. Although you are the one who decides how long your book stays in print, consider these questions.

Do I have time? Local and national promotion can be very time consuming. Also, consider the time factor for other questions.

What plan can I develop for national distribution? Some self-published books succeed in catalogs, independent book stores, on the Internet, etc. I have made sales to publishers, but my plan to self-publish started when I met two authors whose successful self-published books were in many of the catalogs which came to my office where I worked as a school counselor and school psychologist. I wrote *Little Lemon: Activities for Developing Motivation and Memory Skills* which is now in an educational catalog. It is very different from anything I have sent to trade publishers.

How is my type of book marketed? Self-help, inspirational, how-to, and educational books tend to be some of the more successful self-published books. Many books find a welcome audience through national groups dealing with their specialty areas.

How are my skills for writing, editing, and proof-reading? Each requires different skills. Editing and proof-reading require a level of objectivity and attention to detail which many writers do not like.

Do I know how to run a small business? You can take courses through the small business administration and get software such as Quick Books to help you with record keeping.

How are my management skills? If you do not have good ones, learn them from books or courses.

Am I a sales person? You can read books or take courses about selling. You might get training by working in a sales department or by selling a product on commission.

Do I believe in my product enough to do a lot of promotion? You can make many local sales and regional sales if you have time.

Can I sell enough books to cover printing costs and make a profit? For information about publishing, trade shows, etc., contact The Publishers Marketing Association, The Small Publishers Association of North America, Open Horizons, and Para Publishing. (Appendix A) Read books by Dan Poynter and John Kremer. (Appendix B) Learn about e-publishing and print-on-demand. Promotion and distribution can be expensive. Bookstores, catalogs, etc. take 40%-55% of the retail price. Be sure to buy a set of ISBN's and a bar code.

How much will I pay an artist? An artist might work for a flat (one-time) fee or for an advance which is applied to a 5% royalty.

What will the total cost be? Contact book manufacturers who have reputations for quality. For good ones, consult *The Literary Market Place* found in most libraries. Get samples and estimates from more than one company. Price depends on the paper size and thickness, the number of colors and illustrations, the number of books, the type of cover, etc. If you sign a contract, they make up a proof for your approval before the book is printed.

Self-publishing can be successful but consider carefully if it is right for you and right for the type of book you have written.

11. What Should I Know about Copyright?

Text and art work are protected by the copyright law as soon as they are in tangible form. Rough drafts, rejection slips, notes from writers, etc. can document this. If you need to sue for infringement, register with the copyright office before legal action begins. (Address is in Appendix A) Your rights are still protected even if the infringement took place before registration. Publishers generally register copyrights for their writers and artists.

The SCBWI recommends using copyright notice on works you submit. Forms of the notice are: c 1999 Betsy B. Lee, Copyright 1999 Betsy B. Lee, or Copr. 1999 Betsy B. Lee. You do not have to re-register when your work is published, but it is a good idea.

Regarding fair use, you may quote fifty to 200 words without permission. This does not apply to brief material such as poetry or song lyrics. In some cases, you will have to seek permissions and pay fees. Before signing, be sure you understand your contract. (Seuling, Appendix B) The law is open to interpretation sometimes. Your publisher has experts, but you must supply accurate information.

Titles, names, short phrases, slogans, and lists of contents may not be copyrighted. Some titles and names are protected by Trademark.

Your own copyright is bought in most work for hire contracts. You cannot use the material again and you usually are paid one flat-fee.

In flat-fee contracts, you often retain your copyright or have it returned to you after the work is published.

In a book contract, the publisher controls the rights covered in the contract. Study the contracts carefully. You can request changes.

Most magazines buy first rights. After they publish the story, you can sell it again offering second rights. You keep the copyright.

More details about contracts, rights, etc. are available in writers' magazines, *The Children's Writer's & Illustrator's Market*, and to members of the SCBWI and The Author's Guild. (Appendix A)

12. What Should I Do about Record Keeping?

An itinerary helps you keep track of your stories. Use this method or develop another which works best for you. Create a folder for each story and for each publisher. On the front of the story's folder, make an itinerary. List: Publisher - Date Sent - Postage - Date Returned - Comments. On the front of the publisher's folder, list: Story - Editor - Date Sent - Date Returned - Comments. Be sure to note the name of any editor who makes comments. Try this publisher again. Keep copies of correspondence in the publisher's folder.

Keep track of deductible expenses such as supplies and postage. The IRS might question if your writing is a hobby or a business and not allow deductions for some expenses. Check with resources such Bunnin and Beren (Appendix B), your tax advisor, or the IRS. Tax laws and procedures change and they can be interpreted differently. The reference by Bunnin and Beren also has information about the publishing contract, defamation, copyright, legal resources, etc.

Make an index file for the names and complete contact information of sources. Give each source a number. Put this number on your rough drafts to be sure you remember what information came from each source. Do not include the numbers on the submitted manuscript. You do not use footnotes, but you may need statements such as, John Kremer suggests .... It is better to do this too often than not to do it often enough.

Make a list of your sources to send with your manuscript. This will document your facts. Your publisher is knowledgeable about when you need to ask permission to use material; however, you are responsible for documenting the sources and providing contact information.

13. How Can I Increase Sales after Publication?

The two valuable books on this topic are those in Appendix B by John Kremer and by Susan Raab. Unless stated otherwise, the advice which is presented here is in both sources.
Coordinate all of your efforts for publicity by communicating with your publisher. Take the initiative. Publishers spend more of their time and money on big names than on newcomers. (Raab) Speak at schools. Teach a course. Do a workshop. Speak to clubs and other groups which might have a special interest in your topic.

I have found that many authors sell their books on their web sites through online bookstores. On your web site, include information about workshops you can offer for school visits and other occasions. The SCBWI has links to members' web sites.

Give publicity information to any school you attended and to any town where you used to live. Remember organizations to which you now belong or ones to which you used to belong. High schools and colleges are interested in spreading news about their graduates. Let your elementary school know about your children's book.

Arrange interviews on radio or TV if possible.

John Kremer suggests giving away pens. Business cards are good but they are often put away. People use the pens and see your information often. You can get names of promotional catalogs from schools, service organizations, etc.

Ask your publisher if you may be a distributor. You buy your books at a discount from the publisher; then you resell them getting a commission plus royalties. (Raab)

Sell books at speaking engagements. Carry them when you travel. Look for speciality bookstores or gift shops to carry your books.

You get the best results from publicity done before publication and during the Christmas season. If your book features a different season, start publicity a few weeks before the season begins.

14. What's Next?

Reading this book and taking a course are good beginnings. Some of the next steps which I recommend are to study this book carefully; read several books about writing for children; read many children's books; explore Internet resources for writers; read writers' magazines; subscribe to an online writer's listserve for free; join a writer's critique group; and join the SCBWI.

Keep your writing which you really like especially if you get recognition for it. You could find a new market for it; use it as a spring board for creating a new story, poem, article, or book; revise it and send it out; and keep it to share with children, family, and friends. Continue the work of writing, polishing, and researching markets. While you are waiting to be published, enjoy writing and reading as hobby. However, remain focused.

The sonnet I mentioned in the first chapter earned an A+ in a college English class decades ago. It's long gone. I only remember the last two lines. I have thought of a way I could have used it.

> So now, I wish I'd kept my little sonnet
> And also kept my handy thinking bonnet.

Repeating *my little sonnet* and *my handy thinking bonnet* from my first chapter is a technique called a <u>narrative arc</u>. Words or events can be repeated for a powerful effect. These might evoke sadness, laughter, etc. Narrative arcs are used in fiction and nonfiction to help the reader remember points and/or become more emotionally involved.

Writing, reading, and being with children yields rewarding experiences. May you use the information in this book to develop your own style and productive methods of writing. I hope you reach your goal of being published, and I hope you enjoy the steps along the way.

Appendix A

Writers' Organizations and Magazines

The Authors Guild
330 West 42nd St. (29th Floor), New York, NY 10036
Membership - published authors.   Free info at http://www.authorsguild.org

Children's Book Council
568 Broadway, New York, NY, 10012
(212) 966-1990   http://www.CBCBooks.org
The web site has a list of member publishers and updated submission details.

Society of Children's Book Writers and Illustrators (SCBWI)
8271 Beverly Boulevard, Los Angeles, CA 90048
(323) 782-1010   http://www.scbwi.org
This is the only national association solely for published and unpublished children's writers and illustrators. Members can subscribe to a listserv.

Children's Book Insider
901 Columbia Rd., Fort Collins, CO 80525-1838
(719) 836-0394   editors@write4kids.com   http://www.write4kids.com
Publication with market info and how-to articles. Subscribe to a free listserv.

Children's Writer
93 Long Ridge Road, West Redding, CT 06896
(800) 443-6078   http://www.childrenswriter.com
Monthly newsletter published by The Institute of Children's Literature.

Publishers Weekly
249 West 17th St., New York, NY, 10011
(800) 278-2991
Publishing trends, a section on the juvenile market, etc., available at most libraries.

The Writer, Inc.
120 Boylston St., Boston, MA 02116-4615

Writer's Digest
PO Box 2124, Harlan, IA 51593-2313

Other Resources

American Booksellers Association
828 South Broadway, Tarrytown, NY 10591
Phone: (800) 637-0037, (914) 591-2665   http://web.bookweb.org
Independent bookstores nationwide; BookExpo America book fairs, etc.

Authors and Illustrators for Children Webring
Most sites have free information for beginning writers or illustrators.
                                        http://www.geocities.com/Heartland/Shores/2084

Open Horizons
P.O. Box 205, Fairfield IA 52556
(800) 796-6130   info@bookmarket.com   http://www.bookmarket.com
John Kremer: self-publishing, promotion, and much more.

Para Publishing
530 Ellwood Ridge, Santa Barbara, CA 93117-1047
(805) 968-7277   info@ParaPublishing.com   http://www.parapublishing.com
Dan Poynter: self-publishing, promotion, and much more.

Publishers Marketing Association (PMA)
627 Aviation Way, Manhattan Beach, CA 90266
(310) 372-2732   info@pma-online.org   http://www.pma-online.org
The association of independent publishers. PMA has chapters in many areas.

R.R. Bowker's BookWire   http://www.bookwire.com
Info and links to Publisher's Weekly, School Library Journal, Apply for ISBN/SAN, Assoc. of Authors' Representatives, Inc., Book Industry Study Group, Regional Booksellers Associations Guide, and much more.

R.R. Bowker Catalog   http://www.bowker.com
121 Chanlon Rd., Providence, NJ 07974 (800) 521-8110

The Small Publishers Association of North America (SPAN)
P.O. Box 1306, Buena Vista, CO 81211
(719) 395-4790   span@SPANnet.org   http://www.SPANnet.org

Library of Congress
Copyright Office, 101 Independence Avenue, S. E., Washington, D.C. 20559-6000 Circulars, announcements, regulations, other related materials, and all copyright application forms are available from this address and via the Copyright Office Homepage   http://www.loc.gov/copyright

The online text of the U.S. Copyright law
is in the Adobe Acrobat PDF format at   http://lcweb.loc.gov/copyright/title17
Copyright basics without Adobe at http://www.loc.gov/copyright/circs/circ1.html

Appendix B

Books

1001 Ways to Market Your Books: For Authors and Publishers, John Kremer. Open Horizons, 1998.
This book is highly valued by people who sell to publishers and/or who self-publish.

2000 Poet's Market, Chantelle Bentley. Writer's Digest Books, 1999.
This edition lists hundreds of publishers of poetry, plus information about contests, awards, conferences, workshops, organizations, and web sites.

2000 Children's Writer's & Illustrator's Market, Alice Pope. Writer's Digest Books, 2000.
Lists with contact information for hundreds of publishers, advice about writing, marketing, etc.

An Author's Guide to Children's Book Promotion, Susan Salzman Raab. Raab Associates, 1999.
Learn about working with publishers, getting your book distributed, promoting to schools, libraries, bookstores, etc.

Children's Writer's Word Book, Alijandra Mogilner. Writer's Digest Books,1992.
Graded word lists (K-6), a thesaurus indicating reading levels, advice about word usage, and samples of writing.

Comedy Writing Secrets, Melvin Helitzer. Writer's Digest Books, 1992.

The Complete Rhyming Dictionary, Clement Wood. Doubleday, 1991.
This classic has more than 60,000 entries.

The Craft of Writing the Novel, Phyllis Reynolds Naylor. The Writer, Inc., 1989.

Educational Psychology, Thomas L Good and Jere E. Brophy. Longman, 1990.
Information about Maslow's theory and many other theories of motivation, etc.

Elements of Style, William Strunk and E. B. White. Macmillan, 1979.
This book is recommended in most books about how to write. It covers grammar, punctuation, and many other elements of style.

How to Get Your Teaching Ideas Published, Jean Stangl. Walker & Co., 1994.

How to Write Attention-Grabbing Query & Cover Letters, John Wood. Writer's Digest Books, 1996.
A successful magazine editor shares advice and many sample letters that have succeeded.

How to Write a Children's Book and Get It Published, Barbara Seuling. Macmillan, 1991.
Get the inside picture from an editor/author/illustrator who is on the board of directors of the Society of Children's Book Writers and Illustrators. Contents include: learning your craft; writing picture books, easy readers, chapter books, novels, non-fiction, verse, and plays.

How to Write and Sell Children's Picture Books, Jean E. Karl. Writer's Digest Books, 1994
Learn about creating picture books from an award winning editor/author. Contents include: the skills you need to be successful; writing fiction, non-fiction, poetry, essays, and concept books.

How to Write and Sell Historical Fiction, Persia Wooley. Writer's Digest Books, 1997

How to Write, Illustrate, and Design Children's Books, Frieda Gates. Lloyd-Simone Publishing, 1986

A Piaget Primer: How a Child Thinks, Dorothy G. Singer. Plume, 1996.
Studies about childhood perceptions.

Playwriting: A Complete Guide to Creating Theater, Shelly Frome. McFarland & Company, 1990.

A Poetry Handbook, Mary Oliver. Harcourt Brace, 1995.
A Pulitzer Prize winning poet presents lessons about free verse, sound, line length, meter, breaks, poetic forms, tone, imagery, and more.

Nonfiction Book Proposals Anybody Can Write: How to Get a Contract and an Advance Before Writing Your Book, Elizabeth Lyon. Blue Heron Pub., 2000.
Lyon is an editor and writing instructor who presents practical, clear information with many examples of proposals.

Nonfiction for Children, Ellen E. M. Roberts. Writer's Digest Books, 1986. Unfortunately, this excellent book is out of print. Perhaps, you can get it through the interlibrary loan if your library does not have it. You can try a search for out-of-print books at amazon.com and other places.

The Psychology of Learning, James Deese. McGraw-Hill. 1958. Kurt Lewin, etc.

The Self-Publishing Manual: How to Write, Print and Sell Your Own Book, Dan Poynter. Para Publishing, 1997. Sound advice from someone who has successfully self-published many books.

Techniques of the Selling Writer, Dwight V. Swain. Univ. of OK Press, 1981. This classic is recommended in many books about writing.

World-Building (Science Fiction Writing Series), Stephen L. Gillett, Writer's Digest Books, 1996.

Writer's Digest Handbook of Magazine Article Writing, Jean M. Fredette. Writer's Digest Books, 1990.

A Writer's Guide to a Children's Book Contract, Mary Flower. Fern Hill Books, 1988.

The Writer's Legal Companion: The Complete Handbook for the Working Writer, Brad Bunnin and Peter Beren. Harpercollins, 1998. Professionals in the book business consult this for information about legal issues, contracts, agents, defamation, copyright, taxes, high-tech publishing, etc.

Writing for Children and Teenagers, Lee Wyndham. Writer's Digest, Inc., 1980. This classic was written by an author of numerous books, short stories, articles, and serials. Contents include: many details about how to create realistic characters, dialogue, plot, atmosphere, etc.; organization of your book; techniques for improving the beginning, middle, and end of your story; information about contracts, research, etc.; how to write mystery stories, novels, picture books, easy-to-read and hi-low books, nonfiction, plays, and magazine articles/stories.

Writing Juvenile Stories and Novels, Phyllis A. Whitney. The Writer, Inc., 1976.

Writing the Modern Mystery, Barbara Norville. Writer's Digest Books, 1992.

Writing to Inspire, William Gentz, Lee Roddy, et al. Writer's Digest Books, 1987.

Writing Young Adult Novels, Hadley Irwin and Jeannette Eyerly. Writer's Digest Books, 1988.

Index

agents 12 - 13
AIC Webring 34

beginnings 5, 20, 32
board books 26
book length 9-10

concept books 24-25
conflict 20-21
copyright 29, 34
cover letters 10 - 11

dummy of picture book 15

editorial responses 11 - 12
ending 21
expenses 30

feedback 6, 12, 32
fiction 16-21, 24-25
    Middle grade 26
    Young adult 26
flat fee 28-29
foreshadow 18
format 7, 8

goal 17, 20-21

illustrations 11, 14, 15
itinerary 30

Karl, Jean 15, 24, 36
Kremer, John 28, 31, 35

magazines 9, 13, 23-24, 29, 33
main character 16-19, 21
manuscript
    form 6-7
    number of pages 9-10
middle 20-21
motivation 16 - 17

narrative arc 32
needs 17
nonfiction 5, 22-25
novelty books 26

outline 16, 22-25

permissions 23, 30
perspective 19-20
Piaget, Jean 20, 36
picture books 14-15, 23-26
plants 18
plot 16, 20-21
poetry & verse 26, 35-36
Poynter, Dan 28, 36
promotion 27-28, 31, 33-36

query letters 12, 25, 36

Raab, Susan 29, 35
rights 29

SCBWI 7-13, 29-33
self-publishing 27-28, 33-36
Seuling, Barbara 14-15, 25, 36
show don't tell 19
significance 21
submissions 10 - 11
subsidy publishers 12, 27

tags 18-19
Tarbescu, Edith 14
theme 16
traits 18-19

viewpoint 19
villain 21

work-for-hire 29
writer's block 5